THE
Archive Photographs
SERIES

MARCH

Benjamin Gimbert GC. (1903 - 1976). On Friday, 2 June 1944, Ben Gimbert, with fireman James Nightall, was driving an ammunition train from Whitemoor, March to an American base in East Anglia. As they approached Soham, Ben saw that the first wagon behind the engine was on fire. He stopped carefully and James Nightall detached the burning wagon from the rest of the train. Then they carried on, trying to move the blazing wagon as far from the station and town as possible. However, while still in the station, over five tons of explosive went up killing James Nightall and throwing Ben Gimbert two hundred yards from the engine. Frank Bridges, the signal man at Soham station, was also killed in the explosion. The action of Ben Gimbert and James Nightall meant that the town of Soham, whilst badly damaged, was not destroyed as it would have been if the entire train of fifty-one wagons, approximately four hundred tons, had ignited. Benjamin Gimbert and James Nightall were awarded the George Cross for their efforts. Ben survived the explosion and, after a period of convalescence, returned to light duties on the railway. He proudly displays all of his medals in July 1972, from left to right they are the *Daily Herald* Order of Industrial Heroism, the LNER Gallantry Medal, the George Cross and the Coronation Medal, given after being invited to attend the Coronation in 1953. Later, in recognition of their devotion to duty, British Railways named two Class 47 diesel locomotives after the George Cross winners. (Joyce Dedman Collection)

THE Archive Photographs SERIES

MARCH

Compiled by
Peter Hewitt
Richard Munns
Edna Stacey
Ann Thacker
on behalf of the March and District Museum Society

CHALFORD

First published 1998
Copyright © The March and District Museum Society, 1998

The Chalford Publishing Company
St Mary's Mill, Chalford,
Stroud, Gloucestershire, GL6 8NX

ISBN 0 7524 1095 4

Typesetting and origination by
The Chalford Publishing Company
Printed in Great Britain by
Bailey Print, Dursley, Gloucestershire

West End, March. One of the oldest parts of the town, including houses from the early seventeenth century, still exhibits its charms with gardens which extend down to the river.

Contents

Acknowledgements

The compilers would like to thank those who have, over the years, shown an interest in March by taking photographs of the everyday life of the town and who have donated them to March Museum. The curator's organisation of this collection has facilitated the selection of the photographs and we also thank the committee for their support in this project.

We would also like to thank *The Cambridgeshire Times* who have placed their archives at our disposal to enable us to check the background information on many of the photographs. In addition, thanks are due to those who have helped to identify many individuals in the photographs of groups and events included in the book. While we hope that the information is correct, we would be grateful for any further information regarding any of the illustrations.

Introduction

This collection of photographs, all taken from the March Museum archive, are in the main, published here for the first time. The majority of them date from between 1890 and 1950 and depict both the changing physical scene and the varied activities of the community. Like all small country towns, March has changed greatly in recent years, both in its actual appearance and in the occupational make-up of its population, but photographs of societies and sports teams remind us also of continuity. March earlier this century was a vibrant community with its multiplicity of small private businesses: people shopped in the middle of the town; the streets were often full of people; special occasions were celebrated in great style by everyone and overall the town was the centre of the people's social life. Victor Canning, a well-known journalist of the 1930s described at length his visit in 1936 to March, the 'weekend Mecca of the Fens' and his comments on Saturday night are worth quoting.

'Saturday night! Gala night in March. Into the small town has come a jostling crowd. The streets are packed with a slow-moving, joking, flirting, healthy mob; labourers from the fen farms and hamlets, their good wives..... in they come to seek colour, warmth and laughter. They have come by car, by omnibus, by train, on cycles, in pony-carts, and walking..... farmer's sons, red of face, their checked caps tipped at jaunty angles, girls with complexions that need little cosmetics, housewives bulging with parcels and good humour, and burly labourers, their hands grained with work and soil.'

As Canning goes on to describe, their needs were very well catered for by two cinemas and a great number of pubs, reduced from over seventy at the turn of the century but still well in excess of today's number. Indeed in many ways the 1930s was a vintage decade for the town and its institutions as the illustrations here clearly indicate.

This is not the place for a full historical study of March but it is worth outlining briefly some of the factors in its growth for it is essentially a very linear town. Originally on the northern edge of the island of Doddington a small settlement evolved where a chapelry was established and eventually a township around it. Our greatest historical treasure, St Wendreda's church, with its marvellous angel roof completed in the early sixteenth century, became a place of pilgrimage to the shrine of the saint, although until the middle of the nineteenth century it was still only a chapelry within the parish of Doddington. March's unofficial emblem is the old stone cross in the Avenue, possibly a stopping point for a brief sermon to pilgrims, about half-way between the river and the church.

Gradually, as the River Nene became a trading artery in the sixteenth century and after, the township was pulled towards the river and its northern side. Many fine houses were constructed along High Street, opposite the Hythe, a water course (and later sewer) running parallel to it and into the Nene, with extensive gardens going back to what is now Elwyn Road, while along Nene Parade and West End merchant's houses were built. Many of these properties still survive, albeit much altered. One sign of the increased prosperity was the granting, in 1670, of the right to hold a market.

By the early nineteenth century March had a population of over 5,000 and, just north of the river, Broad Street had evolved as the focal centre for retail trades and economic activity. However, to all intents and purposes the town ended beyond Broad Street. It was the coming of the railway which was to have a dramatic effect on the town's geography. The opening of the Eastern Counties station in 1847 and the subsequent development of March as a junction together with an important locomotive depot, elongated March even more, pulling it further away from its original site at Town End. Station Road first linked the town with the station and then other residential areas followed. With the opening of the huge marshalling yards in 1929-33, at the time the biggest in Europe, the town extended even further and in demographic terms became one of England's railway towns, an oddity in an area otherwise so dominated by agricultural activity. It was largely the railway which brought about a steady population growth and which provided the stimulus for the increasing number of institutions depicted in the following pages. However, it must also be remembered that in 1889 March became the County Town for the newly constituted Isle of Ely which necessitated the building of the County Hall in County Road and which brought in an influx of professional employees.

Now, at the end of the twentieth century, much has gone. The railway and a later station survive, but the marshalling yards and engine sheds have disappeared leaving a large wasteland. The Isle of Ely has long been subsumed into Cambridgeshire but March is still the home of the Fenland District Council. The town currently has no cinema and no large public hall, and most of the old family businesses have come to an end. An impressive high security prison now occupies part of the site of the Whitemoor marshalling yards. Yet it is not good to be nostalgic and suppose all change is unfortunate. As the Millennium comes, March is looking forward with confidence to celebrating it. What this book will do, we hope, is to remind the older reader, and to inform the younger, of one phase, in reality quite a short one, in the history of the community of March.

One
Town Views
North of the River

MARCH 5459

The centre of March, Broad Street, before the First World War. Wide open spaces with little traffic.

Broad Street looking south around the turn of the century. The large house in the foreground was the home of the Sharman family and is now where Woolworth's stands.

Broad Street looking south a few years later, c. 1935. The old George and Star was demolished in 1939. With the outbreak of war, the new building would not have been started if all of the materials had not already been on site. The old Mechanics Institute can be seen on the right where the National Westminster bank now stands.

The war memorial as it originally was in 1929. A few years later it was moved ten feet to accommodate the increase in traffic and placed upon a plinth.

The fountain at the northern end of Broad Street was erected in 1912 to commemorate the coronation of King George V. It was paid for by public subscription and was the cause of much discussion as many people thought it out of place and questioned its usefulness. In its original form it was twenty-two feet high and cost £180.

The Statute Fair in Broad Street in 1910. This fair was *the* fair of March. Many years ago this was the day that farmers hired workmen for the next year.

The Statute Fair in Broad Street in 1950. As the requirement for hiring labourers died out, the fair became just a great day out for children who were given a day off from school. The fair took up the whole of one side of Broad Street and the Market Place. However, in the early 1970s, due to traffic problems, it was moved to the City Road car park.

Darthill House was the home of Mr Wise a local solicitor at the turn of the century. It was an imposing residence looking straight down into Broad Street. Around 1910 it was purchased by the Collingwood family who developed the front garden into shops and a public hall.

The Wheel Inn, c. 1900. It was reputed to have very small rooms with very low ceilings and was demolished around 1980 to make way for flats. R.F. Beriolle, whose shop is on the right, was a local photographer and picture frame maker. He was also the bandmaster for the March Town Band.

Whalebones marked the entrance to the 'Ever Sparkle' aerated water factory in Dartford Road. They were said to have been brought home by a sea captain in the Phillips' family. The fragmented remains of one of them can still be seen today.

Bank House, at the entrance to West End from the town centre, was built by the National Provincial bank over one hundred years ago. It was used as a 'British Restaurant' during the war.

River Nene, March.

Looking west towards the Town Bridge. The Temperance Hotel and the Ship Inn are on the right. Left of the bridge is old Bridge House which fell into the river in 1924.

Acre Mill on the left of the photograph was built by Owen Gray and later bought by Joseph Smith, flour millers. The 'lucam' on the side of the building was to enable sacks of grain and flour to be hoisted in and out of the barges which, in the early years of the mill, was the only heavy transport available. Note the houseboats moored at the quay and the rowing boats for hire.

The cleaning of the river at the beginning of this century and the last time that it was done in this way. Many workers came over from Ireland to do this work as did the original Navigators during Vermuyden's time. It was a long and arduous task but essential to keep the river traffic flowing.

Cleaning the river with a barrow hoist, for removing the spoil, making the work much easier.

Piling the banks at the end of Nene Parade with the help of a stationary steam engine.

Mr R. Sharman and Mr W. Grounds rowing on the river in 1900. Nene Parade cottages are on the left.

The residents of Nene Parade welcome the postman, *c.* 1900.

The 'Nene Paraders' get together for a photograph, *c.* 1900.

Station Road, c. 1900. The railway footbridge can be seen in the distance and on the right are open fields where the residents would go 'gleaning' after the harvest.

The Griffin Hotel wagon on its way to the station in 1910. The Primitive Methodist chapel is on the corner. The shop to the left of the chapel was Crawley's general stores and the cemetery chapel spire can be seen on the right. Road improvements have been carried out with the paths now paved.

T. Cross delivering milk in New Park. The milk was brought in churns and measured into the customer's own jug or bowl. With no refrigeration available, milk was 'scalded' as soon as it was delivered to prevent it souring in hot weather.

March Council carts at Ritchie's coachbuilders, Station Road (now Westgate House). Next to the coachbuilders was a blacksmith and farrier and it is likely that the horses had just received new shoes.

Two
Town Views
South of the River

This Public Room and fire engine house, surmounted by a turret, clock and fire bell, was built on the Market Square in 1839. It had a lock-up and four rooms which were used as wards in the cholera epidemic in 1849. A notice on the centre door housing the fire engine states 'key kept in the Griffin Tap'.

MARCH IN THE ISLE OF ELY CAMBRIDGESHIRE

A print of the old Market Place, *c.* 1800. The market site dates from 1670. The Buttercross had disappeared by the early twentieth century.

Now the Magistrates Court, this was formally the Town Hall, but originally built in 1900 as a Corn Exchange at a cost of £3,000. The copper-clad tower is 110 feet high and contains a clock bought by public subscription to commemorate the diamond jubilee of Queen Victoria. The building on the left belonged to Palmers who produced fins for bombs in the First World War.

The White Hart Hotel in the
1890s at the junction of Nene
Parade and Broad Street.

High Street looking north from the market place. Note the boxes of Sunlight soap and cocoa on
the pavement outside Thorn's shop. The Golden Lion and Thorn's have been combined into
Mitchell's the butchers.

High Street looking south from the bridge. Old Bridge House is on the right, the building on the left was the post office, built in 1887 and closed in 1901 despite much opposition.

High Street in the early 1950s. The metal footway was added to the bridge in 1931 and incorporated, in 1954, into the bridge itself when widened to accommodate the increase in traffic.

High Street looking south in the 1930s.

Looking north from Burrowmoor Road. The house on the right was built in the seventeenth century and occupied by E. Marriott, confectioners. Along the eaves are a number of corbel stones carved with different figureheads. On the chimney stack, below a figurehead, is the inscription 'Here lies John Blake, whose head will never ache'. This is now the site of the TSB bank and the carved corbels survive in March Museum.

Looking south around 1900. The old County Court on the left is now the snooker club. Notice the awnings over the path. Hoppers the blacksmiths was on the right.

Moving further south along High Street is the Cock Inn, on the left, in 1912. Next door is the 'Maze', a house which had an exotic garden. Concerts were held here and the public were allowed to enter free of charge.

Fisher's Corner, Town End. This was the main road into March before Wimblington Road was realigned, c. 1930.

Wimblington Road during realignment. The new road that is being built to the right went through the Town End Pits, only one of which now remains.

Elms in the Avenue. This double row of magnificent trees crossed the area known as 'The Field' towards St Wendreda's church.

Road construction in the Causeway, close to the junction with St Peter's Road, in the 1930s.

Three
Business Life
North of the River

Green's were carpenters and blacksmiths. Situated at the Guide Post in Wisbech Road, it was so named because of the direction sign outside the premises.

The dust cart, outside the Conservative Club, in Creek Road, in the early 1930s. Notice the horse's nosebag hanging on the cart.

The baker and confectioner delivering in Creek Road in 1910. The advantage of horse power for deliveries, meant the roundsman could make his way down the road and the horse would follow, beckoned just by a whistle.

The Co-op baker outside Morton's Granary, Station Road, in 1910.

The Co-op paraffin wagon outside the old Peterborough Equitable and Industrial Co-operative Society shop, Station Road, in 1920. This site is now occupied by Jim Hocking Court. This is a block of flats, named after an Australian pilot in the Second World War who died avoiding crashing on the town. Paraffin was the main fuel for a number of homes in and around March before the wide spread introduction of gas and then electricity.

The Thatch in Dartford Road. Formerly the home of the Pilgrim family who started the garage, now owned by John Brown. The Thatch is reputed to be one of the oldest surviving residences in March.

Jane's shop in the 1970s. This shop on the corner of Dartford Road and Grays Lane is now an Indian restaurant.

Peterborough Co-operative Society in Station Road during the 1930s. On the left was a grocery department, in the centre, drapery, boots and outfitting departments and on the right the butchery. Behind this facade was a complex of stores above which was the Co-op Hall, a popular and well-used meeting room for organisations within the town.

Two satellite shops were established by the Co-op in March to provide for the expanding population of the town. This is the Maple Grove Co-op store in the 1930s.

Sutterby and Gay, Marcam House, Station Road, was both men's and ladies' outfitters, serving the town from the late 1940s to the early 1980s.

Sutterby and Gay advertising the March store. Other stores were located at Wisbech and Spalding.

Station Road before Marcam House was built in the 1930s. Notice that the shops were built in front of houses which are still there. Fells Ltd, the cycle retailer, opened the March shop in 1927.

The small wooden shop in Creek Road run by a Mr A.V.N. Christmas. Notice the cream cakes in the outside display on the pavement.

Thomas Morton, corn, cake and seed merchant, produced several kinds of meal and foodstuffs for livestock. Situated at the junction of Station Road and St Johns Road, the granary was demolished in the late 1980s to make way for flats.

G.S. Mitchell's shop and post office in Station Road in 1927. They first used the shop on the opposite corner with County Road and later moved to the right hand side. G.S. Mitchell sold the business to F. Brittain in 1957.

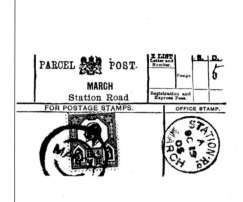

STATION ROAD TSO MARCH, CAMBS

OPENED 1st July, 1891

1900 W. A. MILLER .... Appointed Sub Postmaster
1902 J. N. O. W. MARRIOTT ... Appointed Sub Postmaster
1904 G. SETCHFIELD .... Appointed Sub Postmaster
(above 3 appointments from information in Post Office Records, London)

1916 G. S. MITCHELL ....Sub Postmaster
1925 Post Office transferred to shop opposite side of County Road
1925 G. S. MITCHELL ....Sub Postmaster
(information taken from Kelly's directory)
1957 April 1st F. C. BRITAIN ... Appointed Sub Postmaster
and remained in that position until the Post Office Closed

CLOSED 29th March, 1985

To mark the closure of the post office, on 29 March 1985, a card was produced listing the ninety-four year history of the shop.

STATION ROAD MARCH TSO

Opened 1st July, 1891   Closed 29th March, 1985

An unusual 'last day cover' commemorating the closure of the sub post office in Station Road showing the two shops used on opposite sides of County Road.

The March Motor Co. bus outside the garage in Darthill Road. The Wayman family was one of the first to operate a bus service in the area in the 1920s. The garage was demolished in 1996.

H. Russell, family grocer at No. 26 Broad Street was managed by Mr Burn, seen on the right, and later it was bought by Lamberts. They traded in the town for over fifty years and their van made weekly deliveries to the outlying fen.

Levitts were high class tailors and could be found in the town from early this century until the 1950s. Originally their premises were in Broad Street, where Mackays have their new store, but for the latter part of their time they moved to Marcam House, Station Road.

Walter Dellar, men's outfitters was a familiar shop in Broad Street from the 1920s until the 1960s. Prices displayed included a jacket for 23s 6d (£1.17p), trousers for 14s 11d (£0.75p) and a greatcoat for 35s (£1.75p).

L. Palmer and Co. was an old established March business and patented an Acetylene Gas Generator 'The Monarch'. An original unit was discovered at Holkham Hall which was returned to March and, after renovation by Esmond Palmer (seen here), grandson of the manufacturer, is now on display at the museum. The Gas Generators were regularly advertised in *The Cambridgeshire Times* in 1912 and provided a means of lighting for houses and farms in the Fen.

'Phone 2179.   Established 1882.   *C.S.*   *May* 19*43*

M*rs* *Connor,*
    8. *Wisbech Road,*   №   309
            March.

Bot. of **W. PALMER & SON** (March) LTD.

Oil and Colour Merchants, Lighting and Heating Engineers, Plumbers and Decorators,

BROAD STREET, MARCH, CAMBS.

A bill heading from W. Palmer & Son, Broad Street, March showing that, although established in 1882, they were still providing a wide range of services in 1943.

The White Hart Buildings. The old hotel was changed into shops and flats in the early 1950s. Haylock's had a china department on the left and a pram shop on the right with Maxey's the estate agents in the middle. In the 1950s, a Silver Cross pram sold for approximately £50. Now the building is occupied by a shoe shop and a betting shop.

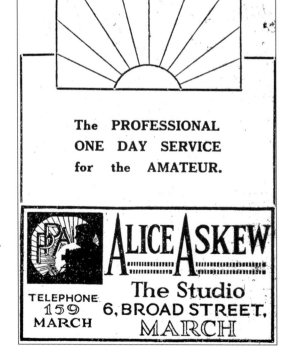

Alice Askew was the best known and the longest lasting of the March photographers. She began her career in 1914, taking over from A.E. Crowson who moved to Bridge House. In the 50s and 60s the shop and studio were occupied by Messers Cochran and Clark. The shop was demolished, together with the old Barclay's bank, to make way for a larger Barclay's building.

The PROFESSIONAL
ONE DAY SERVICE
for the AMATEUR.

ALICE ASKEW

The Studio
TELEPHONE 6, BROAD STREET,
159
MARCH   MARCH

The Easy family had a grocery shop in March and also in Christchurch. The Broad Street shop served the people of March from the mid-30s until the 70s. Their van was a welcome sight in the Fens, delivering groceries and fuel in all weathers. The Ovaltine window display was for a *Daily Express* national competition as part of the 'Help your neighbour' appeal. The poster states 'Every penny spent here helps to reduce unemployment'.

In common with all grocery shops of this time, a number of items were delivered to the shop in bulk. Sugar, dried fruit and butter all had to be weighed out into smaller units before sale. From the bill, dated 5/1/1952, note that ½ lb of Cadbury milk chocolate cost 2/- (10p) and seven cans of 'Kit-e-Kat' were sold for 7/- (5p each), quite an expensive purchase then. Modern prices are, approximately, chocolate at £1.97 and Kit-e-kat 44p a can!

Four

Business Life
South of the River

Burton's Stores and Wine shop were in the High Street for fifty years spanning the war years.
Mr Bert Land (right) stands outside the store at No. 44 High Street in 1929.

The first official March Post Office was built in 1887 on the corner of Elwyn Road and High Street. It contained a public office, dispatch and sorting offices and accommodation for the post master. It closed in 1901 when a new and larger post office was built.

The new post office in Broad Street opened in 1901 and remained until an even larger one was built in Dartford Road, to commemorate the accession to the throne of Edward VIII, in 1936, the king who was never crowned.

J.H. Ladyman were in the town before 1900 and were originally drapers as well as grocers. Lloyds bank took over the premises in the 1950s and only moved from there in 1997.

Edward Charles Haylock established this business, at No. 4 High Street, in 1868. He was a stationer, music and musical instrument seller, piano tuner and teacher of music. The premises were also used as a private school. The last owner, Rupert Haylock, donated a number of display cases to the newly formed March Museum in the 1970s. The 'H' can still be seen in the tiled entrance to Martin's newsagents, the present occupiers.

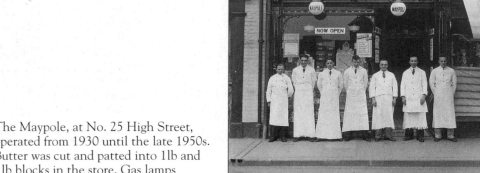

The Maypole, at No. 25 High Street, operated from 1930 until the late 1950s. Butter was cut and patted into 1lb and $\frac{1}{2}$lb blocks in the store. Gas lamps illuminated the front of the window.

Charles Markwell, tailor and hatter, had shops in both the High Street and Broad Street at the turn of the century.

Brown's, drapers and milliners, started in Nene Parade in 1925 and moved to No. 42 High Street in 1929. They employed many young girls and women and also had seamstresses on the premises. Recently demolished, it is now a solicitors and opticians with flats above.

Joseph Smith's granary and mill operated on the Acre Mill site for almost one hundred years. The site was purchased in 1840 by John Smith and, in 1847, he built the first steam powered mill in March. Even small companies took a great pride in their horses and carts which, apart from barges on the river, were the only form of heavy transport available.

Thomas Read and Son, forage merchants, operated in the town until the 1950s. Motor power has now replaced horses but the new lorry is still well looked after. His warehouse was in the Causeway and was reputed to have been the home for the Cavalry horses. This site was until recently Causeway Garage.

Joseph Hopper was a blacksmith and ironmonger in High Street. He also sold agricultural implements. The photograph shows a range of binders, horse ploughs and horse drags from the end of the last century.

Swann's, wheelwrights, traded for many years and over several generations. They were to be found at Town End, opposite the Seven Stars public house. These premises were demolished in 1997.

Joe Setchell was a local dairyman from the mid-1920s until the late 1960s. When Joe first started his business milk was delivered in churns and ladled out to the customer. The farm became the Dairyfields Estate off Burrowmoor Road.

NEW MILK, CREAM
and
NEW LAID EGGS
DELIVERED TWICE DAILY.

J. SETCHELL & CO.

 Burrowmoor Dairy,
MARCH.

Joe Setchell's business card emphasising two daily deliveries.

Harry Burton from Hatchwoods Dairy, Knight's End outside the new Burrowmoor School in 1909.

Elsie Palmer's grocers, tobacconists and sweet shop at No. 67 High Street was the regular haunt for all the schoolchildren in the area, where they would spend their halfpennies and farthings. This shop is now a Chinese take-away.

Coy's harness and saddle makers shop was on the site of what is now Butler's butchers shop in the High Street. The butcher's shop owned by Harradine was there in 1908 (according to the Kelly's Directory).

Ray Hopper outside the family grocery shop started by his parents in 1916. Now the Citizens Advice Bureau.

Ramsdale, fancy drapers and agents for Sketchley Dye Works, could be found on the corner of High Street and Bevill's Place in the late nineteenth century.

Rose's Garage, on the corner of the Causeway and St Peter's Road, is noted for the penny-farthing bicycle displayed on its roof. Horace Rose, the son of the proprietor, was a well-known motor cyclist who competed in the Isle of Man races.

William Baker launched this business in the late 1920s. It became a sub post office in 1929. It was renamed Baker and Edgoose (grocers) in 1947 and, in 1971, Edgoose Carpets, still retaining its sub post office.

Nellie Christmas's shop in the early 1950s. High class ladies fashions and millinery were sold here together with baby's clothing. Situated between the King William IV and Edgoose's shop, it was purchased in 1980 for Susan Edgoose who continued to sell millinery and outsize fashions until changing to rugs and curtains in 1990.

Five
Public Houses

The Wheel Inn in the early 1970s, prior to demolition. This inn was situated on the corner of Robingoodfellows Lane and Station Road and was one of the oldest pubs in the town. Some of the ceilings were so low that a tall person had to stoop when inside.

The Chequers, dating from the early nineteenth century, could be found on the corner of Broad Street and Dartford Road. Here it is decorated for the celebration of the coronation of King George VI and Queen Elizabeth in 1937.

The first George and Star in the early twentieth century. There was a slaughter house located behind the public house. When the pub was demolished, in 1939, a well was found under the foundations which contained a large and very old water jug.

The new George and Star built in 1939 at the commencement of the Second World War. It is unlikely that this establishment would have been started if the materials for its construction had not already been on the site when war was declared. It was demolished in the early 1990s to make way for a new store and Fenland Walk.

The Prince of Wales in Station Road was demolished in 1977 to enlarge the garden of a house in Milner Close.

The Sun Inn in Nene Parade. This was owned by Ogden & Sons, a local brewery.

The Old Crown Inn was also in Nene Parade. This area was alongside the river and many small alehouses developed to satisfy the thirst of the bargees. In the mid-nineteenth century there were seventy-two recorded public houses in March. It was quite normal to drink ale, which had a very low alcohol content, at all times of day as water was often not fit to drink.

The White Hart Inn was on the corner of Nene Parade and Broad Street. It came into its own when the railway arrived in March. It had its own wagon which transported customers to and from the station. The building was converted to shops and flats in the 1950s.

The Griffin is the oldest hostelry in March. It dates from 1793 as a coaching inn with the 'Posting House', the Mail Coach, arriving daily from London. It had its own brewery on site and was the meeting place for the churchwardens. The Griffin also had its own wagon for visitors travelling by rail.

The White Lion, demolished in the 1970s, could be found at the junction of High Street and St Peter's Road, formerly White Lion Lane. The last licensee was Mrs Bates who always wore a long black skirt and white, high necked blouse.

The Meeting of the Signs

'Twas the **Prince of Wales** who first caught my eye,
On a Galloping Dicky, **Lord Nelson** rode by;
King William the Fourth and the **Georges** were chums,
They saluted the people and twiddled their thumbs.

Then the **Jack of Trumps** came along on a **Wheel**,
Said he, 'I've **Three Fishes** to make me a meal';
Robin Hood who we know had a **Chequer**'d career,
Had scarcely a **Rag** to his back, poor dear.

Yet he wagered a **Crown** that a deal he'd arrange
Which would give him the best in the **Royal Exchange**;
Then a smart **Horse and Jockey** came up like the wind,
Said the rider, 'We left the **White Horse** far behind,
But he'd no doubt arrive before the **Cock** crows.'
Then the **Bull** raised a laugh by blowing his nose.
Quoth the **Griffin**, 'You've a terrible cold I can see,
What say you to a drop of my prime O.B.G.?'

The **White Hart** so sleek and glossy, no doubt
Felt nervous with so many **Lions** about.
In colour they ranged between **Red, White and Golden**,
And looked savage enough to frighten the Old'un.

The **White Swan** now timidly slips down the brink,
Wades into the water and has a good drink.
The **Windmill** just jauntily lift its sails,

In saluting **Three Horseshoes** without any nails
The bold **Pig and Whistle** here started a jig,
When someone cried, 'Stop it, d'ye hear Mr. Pig!'

'I've a toast to propose.' Said Monsieur **Boot and Shoe**.
'Here's the best of good luck to our **Ships, Old and New**
May they amongst foes an **Anchor** ne'er cast,
But peacefully **Plough** the broad ocean so vast,
With them we can always despise war's alarms,
And there's sinew and strength in our **Coachmaker's Arms**.

Our **Carpenter's Arms** too possess enough muscle
To make matters warm if it comes to a tussle!'

On drinking this toast they used **Three Tuns** of sherry,
So you're sure that the party became a bit merry;
They shouted as if opposition to drown,
'The **Shamrock and Thistle**, the **Red Rose and Crown**.'
And ended by toasting each other in whisky,
Till the whole blessed lot were decidedly frisky.

Then the **Sun** gave a hint that he shortly would rise,
I could no longer see **Seven Stars** in the skies;
So yelling and whooping the party dispersed,
To become welcome signs to the people who thirst.

Henry Tipple, 27 March 1899

Six
Railways in March

Class D16 number 62610, approaching March Station, platform two, with a local passenger train from Ely. This engine, of a type well known in the area, was built at Stratford in August 1911 and was eventually scrapped in June 1957. Unfortunately no examples of these 'Claud Hamiltons' have been preserved. The crowded goods sidings indicate the volume of traffic being carried in the late 1940s and early 1950s. The lattice work footbridge and station building to the right have since been demolished.

March Station at the turn of the century with platforms one and two to the right and platforms five and six to the left. The Great Eastern Railway destination board shows the wide range of towns covered by the railway. Note that station shunting of wagons and coaches is being carried out by horse power, well before the introduction of diesel shunters.

March Station, 1905. A 2-4-0 engine number 777 waits with a fast passenger train, probably for Ely. This engine, built at Stratford in June 1892 as Great Eastern Class T19 No 787, was renumbered 777 in April 1904. Many locomotives of this type were converted to 4-4-0 type and this one was rebuilt in 1906.

March was a very large station at the junction of three lines; the GN & GE Joint to Spalding and Doncaster, the Wisbech to St Ives and Cambridge and the Ely to the Peterborough line. In addition to the four main platforms there were three bays at the far (west) end, two between platforms two and five and a third beside platform six. An 'avoiding' line ran round the back of the station to allow freight trains access to Whitemoor marshalling yards without having to pass through the station itself.

The Eastern Counties Railway station, originally built for the coming of the railway to March in 1847, was located in the house on the right which has now become the station master's house with the building of the 'new' station to accommodate the increased amount of passenger traffic. This new station, with an elaborate canopy over the entrance, can be seen to the left and was opened on 23 November 1885. The original station was demolished in 1988 to make way for a business centre.

An Ogden family group outside the station entrance prior to 1914. The two ladies are Lucy Thorn (right) and Mrs T. P. Ogden. Vic Ogden, wearing a cap on the right, is with Tom Parkinson Ogden, wearing a trilby, and behind him, also in a trilby, can be seen John Ogden. Note the horse-drawn bus for 'Ye Old Griffin Hotel', the decoration round the canopy of the station entrance and the fine gas lamp.

Thirty members of the station staff pose for their photograph outside the station. The majority are proudly wearing their GER cap badges which dates the photograph to pre-1923. The two gentlemen in trilby hats, Mr E. Reynolds (second left) who later became station master at Cambridge and Mr D.E. Franklin (fourth from the left) were responsible for the 'strawberry trains' which ran from Wisbech to March and then on to the London market.

Horse power was used for local shunting of wagons and for the delivery of goods arriving by rail.
These proud handlers and stable girls show off their magnificent horses, probably in the 1930s.
The stables were later converted to a clubroom for the British Railways Staff Association.

At the entrance to the station yard, the Temperance Hotel offered 'good stabling and loose
boxes'. The gates to the right of the building were a feature of all railway property. These gates
were closed annually to preserve the private nature of the railway and to prevent a public right
of way being established.

During the Second World War a large number of what had been previously regarded as men's jobs had to be performed by women. Here a group are employed on track maintenance. It was reported in the local paper (27 February 1942) that these twelve women had been employed since the last day of 1941 working from 7.20 a.m. to 5 p.m., being allowed an hour for dinner. Part of their work involved cleaning and oiling the points, 'of which there are 700 sets in the Whitemoor Yard'. 'Inspector B. Greengrass, who is in charge of them, is full of praise for the work they are doing. "They are perfectly happy," he said, "and are very willing and obliging."'

In 1926, with the increase in the amount of traffic being handled, £43,000 was invested in the March Locomotive Depot. Included in this upgrading was the construction of the Coaling Plant, first used on 27 March 1927. Here wagons loaded with coal are being hoisted up the side of the tower for their contents to be tipped into a 500 ton hopper. When an engine required more coal, it would be run under the tower and, in two minutes, five ton could be dropped into the tender. Prior to this technological advance, all refuelling had to be carried out manually. When steam power eventually gave way to diesel, the Coaling Tower was demolished (on the fifth attempt) in July 1966.

At the height of the steam era, nearly 200 engines were based at March. The early Great Eastern Railway locomotive shed, shown here, as it was about to be demolished, was a fine example of late Victorian industrial architecture.

The entrance to the locomotive depot and Whitemoor marshalling yard, as well as the lines to Spalding and Wisbech, were controlled from a single signal box, Whitemoor Junction. This is an interior view showing some of the 147 levers needed to operate the points and signals. This signal box was one of the biggest in the area and two diagram boards, which may be seen on the wall, were needed to allow the men to operate the box safely. The signal levers themselves were unusual in that they were manufactured by Dutton's and were reclaimed from another signal box.

With March at the junction of a number of lines and between Fenland and the Midlands, a large number of freight trains arrived which required sorting for onward shipment. In the early years all this was carried out 'on the flat' by using engines but in 1929 a new system of gravity sorting was installed at a cost of £300,000. A shunter would uncouple the wagons for specific destinations, write out a 'cut-card' as to how many wagons were uncoupled and the train would then be gently pushed up an incline or 'hump'. When the loose wagons reached to top of the hump they would accelerate under gravity and separate from the rest of the train. A controller, who would have received the 'cut-card' from the shunter, would then operate the point switches on the diagram panel in front of him to direct the wagons into one of the forty-two sidings available. This system was so successful that the following year another £300,000 was invested in the building of a duplicate hump to handle 'down' traffic from which this photograph was taken.

An aerial view of the Whitemoor Marshalling yards showing the 'up hump' in the left middle distance and the 'down hump' on the right. The control tower for the up hump can be seen where the lines come together before fanning out again. The Coaling Tower is easily visible, left centre, with the 1930s LNER engine shed to its left and the GER engine shed on the left edge.

Seven
Schools and Education

The South District School was built in 1851 on the site of earlier almshouses and is of Carstone from West Norfolk. It seems originally to have been a private girls' 'grammar school' but in the 1870s became one of the town's two board schools for children from the age of five upwards. Eventually it became the South District Infants school and finally, after closure as a school in 1976, the March and District Museum.

This, and the photograph below, are both taken in the back yard of the South District school about 1900. It would appear to be a May day photograph in view of the garlands. In the four classrooms at that time there was a total of 593 pupils on the registers; 200 girls, 170 boys and 223 infants!

A carefully staged tableau by a group of the older girls. Note the buildings behind both these photographs. These were part of the run-down area of Little London where the City Road car parks now stand.

The top class of infants outside the front of the South District school in 1947 dressed to represent nursery rhymes. By then the children moved on to the Burrowmoor Road school at the age of eight. The school had no grass playing space and was in the middle of the town; far from ideal by the time of its closure.

In common with most small towns, March had several private schools during the nineteenth century. This illustration shows Miss Susan Pope's school at the 'Laurels' in the High Street about 1880. It was obviously well regarded as the pupils came from many of the town's leading families. Back row, left to right: Beatrice Bennet, Violet Aveling, Ida Bondfield, Gertie Sharman, Ethel Bates, May Woolhouse, Ada Johnson. Middle row: Margery Grounds, Ruth Ogden, Ethel Pilling, Laura Bates, John Ogden, Nellie Grounds, Mary Ogden, Maggie Bates, Nora Johnson. Front row: Victor Ogden, Mabel Unwin, Fanny Grounds, Louise Johnson, John Crisp.

In 1827 the Guildhall was built in the High Street in part to house a new National School which, until the 1850s, was the principal school in the town, even incorporating the practically defunct grammar school. This view of about 1880 shows a group of pupils with the teacher, Miss Jackson. Contrast the appearance of the children here with those in the previous photograph.

One of the tiered classrooms in the National school. The 'tiering' arrangement and simple benches enabled large numbers of pupils to be taught and kept under control. The Guildhall later became Bodger's agricultural sales, more recently a bed centre and is now sadly empty and with an uncertain future.

The North District School was built in Dartford Road following the 1870 Education Act as a Board school for the developing town north of the river. The seven classrooms had 758 pupils on the registers in 1902 which is about the time this photograph was taken. This group of forty is probably one class. They are smart but not very cheerful!

A delightful view of one of the classrooms at the North District school about 1914. Note the double desks and the counting skittles. In 1934, the school was designated for infants only and finally closed in the 1980s with the opening of the Maple Grove school. Today it is a business centre.

The opening ceremony in March 1909 of the new South District school in Burrowmoor Road with an impressive line-up of pupils and local dignitaries. This was to be the town's school for 'senior' pupils (i.e. children aged ten years and upward). It was a splendid modern complex and is still functioning as the Burrowmoor Primary school.

A group of senior girls at the South District school in 1922. Most pupils were leaving school well before the official leaving age of fourteen and this is really a very small group considering the overall numbers in the school.

March Grammar School was founded by bequests in 1696 and 1717 by William Neale and Thomas Wade respectively. However, it did not develop any real strength until late in the nineteenth century when it moved from premises in West End to the purpose built property in Station Road, opened in 1876. When this photograph was taken, in 1909, there were approximately eighty-five boys on the roll.

Some seventy-five boys are shown on this photograph of 1910 with five staff and the headmaster, Revd T. Ford. It was taken on the steps of the recently built extension beside Robingoodfellows Lane. This part of the building alone survives in an educational context as the present Community Education Centre.

Following the 1902 Education Act, the Isle of Ely County Council set up a High School for girls and, after using temporary accommodation for three years, the school was opened in County Road in 1909. It had a similar roll to the Grammar school with which it merged in 1969. The building was then taken over by the Hereward schools until the mid-1980s when, after lying derelict for some time, it was demolished to the shame of the town which lost a splendid public hall in the process.

The Hereward school building when opened in 1934. This comprised separate boy's (right) and girls' (left) schools with a common entrance and hall. With single storey classrooms arranged round two quadrangles it represented the very latest in school design. From its opening, the majority of March's youngsters from the age of eleven were educated here. The two schools (boys and girls) were merged in 1969 and, in 1983, all secondary education was moved to the Neale-Wade comprehensive school at the other end of the town. The Hereward school buildings have now also been demolished.

Eight
Notable Buildings

The Market Place, c. 1900. This has been a market site since 1670. The Urban District Council obtained the market rights from the lord of the manor in 1897. On the right is the new corn exchange with its clock tower 110ft high. The clock was a gift from the people of March to celebrate the diamond jubilee of Queen Victoria. The building also housed the town's fire engine.

The Electric Picture Palace was opened in August 1912. It was a well equipped place of amusement and gave two showings per evening. It showed a pictorial record of current events and the programme was changed twice weekly. The pianist was Madam Coleridge LRAM and hardly a vacant seat could be found at any time during performances. This building still stands and can be seen at the top of Robingoodfellows Lane.

The Hippodrome, in Dartford Road, was opened on 8 February 1929. It was built by Eggitt and Son, who were local builders, at a cost of more than £20,000, as a cinema but was used for other entertainment and latterly as a bingo hall. The monogram MA (March Amusements) is still visible above the entrance.

The Regent Theatre, in Robingoodfellows Lane, was used for the first time on 17 April 1895. It was built on the site of a disused malt house to the rear of the Wheel inn. It later became a cinema and the Marcam Hall night club. It was destroyed by fire on New Years Day 1978.

The Regent Theatre had a commodious and imposing interior. It had a large stage with pot plants supplied by Ravenhill, a local nurseryman. The first concert was for the 'Beautification of St Mary's Church Chancel'. Local talent was used for sketches, songs, and pianoforte solos. The cost of the seating was 1/- (5p), 6d and 3d.

Oakwood House in West End was for a number of years the local youth centre. It was demolished to make way for a new health centre in the mid-1960s.

The opening of the new Trustees Savings Bank which came to the town in 1936 in premises overlooking the market place. The bank later moved to High Street next to St Peter's Church.

Work is in hand after a terrible south west gale of hurricane force uprooted trees and damaged property, including the pinnacle of St Wendreda's Church, in 1895.

The Centenary Baptist church, in High Street, was built in just eight months in 1870. It cost £4,600 to build and had, at that time, 670 worshippers. In 1959 it was destroyed by fire and has subsequently been rebuilt.

In 1899 a new Corn Exchange was erected on the Market Place. The framework for the tower was built by A. Christmas & Son, carpenters. To make its construction easier, it was built in their St Peter's Road workshop and then dismantled to be reassembled on site; an early form of pre-fabrication.

The inside of the Hythe. This former waterway was probably Saxon in origin. It was bricked over and enclosed after the great cholera epidemic in 1849. The original watercourse was wide enough to take barges and started at the north west corner of Broad Street and continued southwards as far as Town End.

The band pavilion in the Gaul Road recreation field in the 1930s. It was used for church services and band concerts.

The stone cross in the Avenue, seen here in the early 1930s, was a wayfarer's preaching cross and possibly the site of a Saxon market. The avenue of elms led to S. Wendreda's church.

White's Cottage, *c.* 1880. This cottage was on the corner of Bell Metal Lane (Elwyn Road) and High Street. The White family were basket makers. The cottage was demolished in 1886 to make way for March's first official post office.

Southwell's Mill was to be found in Norwood Road behind where the 'Men of March' now stands. Owned by the Smith family, it was used as a slaughter house until just after the Second World War. It was demolished in 1986.

Nine
People of the Town

Residents of the Jenyns Almshouses in the Avenue, *c.* 1904. The almshouses were built in 1851 by March Consolidated Charities to accommodate four poor widows and four poor men. The almshouses are one of only two buildings in March constructed with Carstone, a dark red sandstone from Norfolk.

Mrs Emery a character from the past. Mrs Emery sold vegetables from house to house around the turn of the century.

Billy Mason was educated at Wisbech Grammar school and was the brother of a doctor. A family quarrel brought him to March where he was to spend the rest of his life. He worked as a drover and general help for local farmers and business men. When he died he was to be given a pauper's funeral but the town decided otherwise. Two prominent townspeople collected enough money from the people of March to give him the funeral he deserved.

Henry Amos lived in Creek Road and was a well-known amateur photographer. He took many photographs between 1880 and 1910; some of which have been donated to the local museum.

Tom Moss the milkman in 1929. One of the many local milkmen who regularly supplied the people of March with fresh milk.

Mr C .H. Wooten of Church Street in 1930. A familiar figure on his cycle and a well known and respected local preacher. For twenty-two years, Mr Wooten cycled on Sundays from March to Welches Dam, where he held Sunday school and took the evening service in the Mission church. Unfortunately on 3 December 1933, whilst cycling into a strong, bitterly cold wind, he collapsed and died half way to Manea.

Dr Alfred Charles Stanley Waters who lived at Hythe House, High Street, dressed for a pageant at Doddington Rectory. He was a local physician and surgeon also secretary for the Isle of Ely BMA and honorary medical officer for the March LNER Ambulance Brigade.

James Cornwell began his business as a
basket maker in 1916 in premises in
Deerfield Road later moving to
Badgeney Road. In 1929, James
Cornwell and Son started to make
canvas toolbags for the railwaymen
who had recently moved into the area.
The factory closed in the early 1940s.

Joseph Hand Jackson and his wife, Emma. Joseph was the headmaster of the British school for
boys and girls at the Guildhall in the High Street in 1875.

Miss Lavinia Peckett in 1933. Miss Peckett, at sixteen, was crowned as the first March Railway Queen; previously the Railway Queen had represented the whole of the Isle of Ely.

The final act of Lavinia Peckett's reign was the crowning the 1934 Railway Queen, Miss May Barker. She went on to represent March in the National Railway Queen Competition in Manchester.

Ten
Events and Celebrations

The March celebrations for the Coronation of King Edward VII in 1902. Ox roasts were quite often the public way of enjoying themselves on such occasions. In charge of proceedings was Mr Birch. The butchers were A. Harradine, S. Wright, W. Edwards and J. Alterton and the spit was built by R. Farrinton and H. Spragg.

The decoration of March Town Bridge for the celebration of the Diamond Jubilee of Queen Victoria in 1897.

The Market Square is decked out on the occasion of King Edward VII's Coronation in 1902. The banner proclaims 'May heaven protect their Majesties'.

March Horse & Foal Show   21.7.1914.

Agricultural shows were very popular in the early part of the century. The first aircraft to be seen in March was on display at the March Horse and Foal Show on the Gaul Road Recreation Field on 21 July 1914.

The unveiling of the war memorial on 19 June 1921. The obelisk is made of Cornish granite and the soldier is carved from a single block of Carrara marble. The original cost of the memorial was £900. The names of the two hundred and ten men of March who were killed on active duty in the First World War were inscribed on it.

The Silver Jubilee of King George V in 1935. A free diner for the old people and unemployed of the town was held in Wayman's garage, situated in Robingoodfellows Lane. Approximately 800 persons attended and two sittings had to be arranged at 12.30p.m. and 1.30p.m.

The Belisha Beacon Boy's Jazz Band, 6 May 1935. They were awarded a special group prize during the celebrations of George V's Silver Jubilee. The costumes, in yellow and black like the Belisha Beacon poles, were handmade by Mrs Hayward and Mrs Wright.

The coronation day of King George VI, May 1937. The crown on March Bridge was made by Turner and Son, carpenters of City Road, who have been established in the town since 1889. The crown, a representation of the imperial state crown, was made in two halves and then assembled on the Market Place before being lifted into position in the early hours of a Monday morning. It was a very large structure, measuring 18ft 3in high, 20ft 6in in diameter and weighing almost 17cwt (850kg).

All over the country, towns and villages celebrated the Coronation of Queen Elizabeth II with street parties. March was no exception with Eastwood Avenue children sitting down to tea, served by their mothers.

SUNDAY, MAY 1st, 1938
at 3 p.m.

DIVINE SERVICE

IN THE RING OF

Bertram Mills' Tenting
Circus at MARCH

For the Artistes and Staff and to
which the Public are cordially invited

Conducted by

The Reverend R. J. P. PEYTON-BURBERY, M.A., R.N.

Assisted by

The Reverend ARTHUR DONALD LAWSON, G.C.M.
Vicar of Wallaby, Lincs.,
and Hon. Chaplain to the Touring Circus.

Choir drawn from the March Churches
and the March Musical Society.

The Hymns will be accompanied by the Circus Orchestra, under
the direction of Jack Lindsley, also by the March Town Silver
Band and the March Railway Silver Prize Band.

A Collection will be taken on behalf of the North Cambs. Hospital,
Wisbech and the Denville Hall, Northwood.

On Sunday 1 May 1938, a divine service was held for the artistes and staff of Bertram Mills' tenting circus. The service was attended by a congregation of 5,000 with more than a thousand turned away. The Revd R.J.P. Peyton-Burbury, Rector of St Mary's delivered his address from the ring.

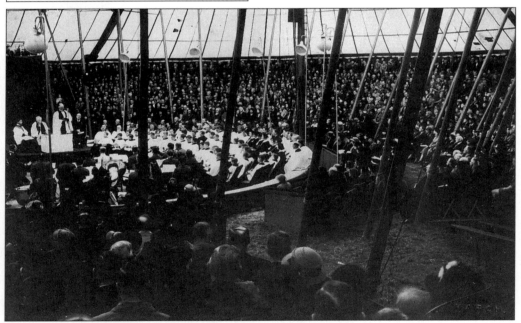

For three days in 1938 Bertram Mills circus came to March. They put up the big top which seated almost 4,000 people on the field which is now Oaktree Close, behind the Jack of Trumps public house. So popular was the circus that people were turned away at every performance. The attendance for the service was the largest ever known for any such 'big top' event.

Peace Day Rally in the GER sports field, June 1919. The large banner comes from the National Federation of Discharged and Demobilised Sailors and Solders, March Branch. The small placard on the right details the carnage during the war with figures of 686,623 killed and 2,049,199 wounded.

An ox roast on the market place for the coronation of George VI in May 1937.

The NALGO (County Hall staff) entry 'Pillars of the Throne' in the float procession for the coronation of Her Majesty Queen Elizabeth, June 1953.

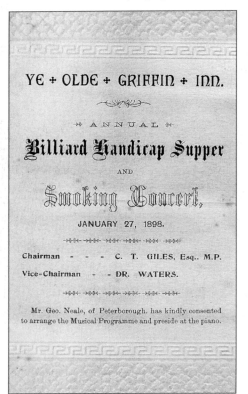

YE ✤ OLDE ✤ GRIFFIN ✤ INN.

✳ A N N U A L ✳

Billiard Handicap Supper

AND

Smoking Concert,

JANUARY 27, 1898.

Chairman - - - C. T. GILES, Esq., M.P.

Vice-Chairman - - DR. WATERS.

Mr. Geo. Neale, of Peterborough, has kindly consented to arrange the Musical Programme and preside at the piano.

What may now be considered to be an unusual event was the Annual Billiard Handicap Supper and Smoking Concert held at 'Ye Olde Griffin Inn' on 27 January 1898. Mixed among numerous toasts and responses were songs including those listed as comic or humourous.

Eleven
Sporting Events

A local police tug-o'-war team is shown with the trophy which they have just won. The photograph, taken early this century, is typical of the high regard that sporting achievements received.

Cricket has featured prominently in the life of March over the years. One of the earliest photographs shows the participants in the third annual match between the T.T. Peyton's Veterans and March Town on 16 June 1908. The Revd Peyton's side contained fifteen players whilst March fielded only fourteen. Batting first, starting at 11a.m., the Veterans declared at 4.30 p.m. allowing the Town less than two hours in which to score the runs. Mr F.D. Grounds, for the Town, was the most successful batsman with seventy-nine not out.

Moving on in time, we now see the club photograph of the under 30s against the over 30s match in 1923. Back row: T.J. Lewis (scorer), -?-, E. Morton, Dr Ling, E. Phillips, W.H. Mitcham, C. Johnson, -?- . Middle row: W. Johnson (umpire), -?-, B. Aveling, C. Sole, ? Shaw, C. Butt, ? Shaw, H.R. Edwards, J. Berry and W. Hay (umpire). Front row: J. Sole, T. Nurse, W. Phillips, E. Johnson, A. Johnson, F.D. Grounds, F. Gutterige and F. Johnson.

March Town First XI of 1950. March Cricket Club had moved from the Estover Road ground to the Avenue sports field. Here we see, back row: C. Parsons, -?- , C. Kisby, W. Shepperson, T.J. Lewis (secretary), D. Clarke, D. Aveling, C. Richmond (scorer and later groundsman). Front row: ? Laver (groundsman), E. Golden, J. Shepperson, Mr Morton, E. Burton, M. Crouch, F. Onion.

Football has been played in March for a long time. This is one of the earliest photographs showing the March team of 1898-9 taken outside Estover House. Unfortunately the names of the players have been lost.

The 1906-7 season proved to be a very successful one for the March Town side as they were winners of the Isle of Ely Cup and champions and holders of the Isle of Ely Junior League. In the photograph we have G.H. Painter (Hon Sec), F.W.M. Powley, T. Love, H. Dicker, E. Gee, C.S. Dicker, A.B. Godfrey, R.J. Caslake, W. Nurse (Capt.), J. Emery. Front row: G. Carmichael and C. Northfield.

The local railway, employing a large number of young men, fielded a successful football team. The March Great Eastern Football Club shows off two trophies at the end of the 1920-21 season. From left to right, back row: Mr W. Stone, F. Bird, G. Munden, H. Bird, W. Morby, T. Cox, C. Morley, H. Wilson (trainer). Middle row: Mr E. Green, W. Whitehead, J. Grainger, H. Dawson, R. Dawson, W. Gutterige, Mr H. Munden. Front row: F. Cousins, Dobson (Mascot), A. Cousins.

March St Wendreda's football team in 1904-5 season. Among the many groups who ran football sides, the churches were well represented. Note the flat caps and the boots without studs!

Also prominent was the St Mary's Football team in 1921. Back row, left to right: Moss, Watson, Unwin, Laws, Saxby, Mortlock and Canon T.T. Peyton. Front row, Hill, Tinkler, Woodhall, Phillips, Spooncer and Fincham with S. Spooncer in front.

The Centenary Baptists' Football Club in 1930-31. This shows that it was not only the Church of England that could field a football team. Careful inspection of the photograph shows that teams were now equipped with studs in their boots. The squad of seventeen was captained by N. Lewis and contained the Revd J.G. Douglas. From the back, left to right: N. Thetford, C. Wright: C.Hudson (ref.), H. Band, K. Barrett, B. Knock, S. Hurst, H. Taylor, J. Atkins, W. Stone (trainer), J. Cox: J. Bales, G. Emery, N. Lewis, G.Afford, J.G. Douglas, B. Plumb, E. Brand, B. Selby, L. Halifax and K. Wallace.

Ladies football is not a modern phenomenon as this photograph shows. The March Ladies FC team of 1932-33 are, back row, left to right: Miss M. Burrell, Miss Barnard, Miss M. Lefrevre, Miss G. Leader, Miss E. Barton, Miss E. Creasey. Front row: -?-, Miss L. Steel, Mrs Legg, Miss J. Frost, Miss M. Harradine. Two games were played against a side from Chatteris. Chatteris won the first, at home, by 3 - 1 but in the return at March the home side were victorious by 9 - 0. The local paper suggested that the improvement in the March performance was due to their chewing gum lasting longer.

104

H. Smith. C. Fox. A. Reynolds. J. Cox, sen. A.C. Turner. G. Marshall.

Photo by R. F. Deriolle. A. Fuller. F. W. Brundell. J. Tyler. C. S. Morris. S. Jackson.

MARCH ANGLING ASSOCIATION.
Winners of March and Wisbech Inter-Club Shield, Seasons 1905, 1906, 1907.

With the large number of rivers and drains in the area, it is not surprising that angling was a favourite pastime for a number of the inhabitants of March. A variety of clubs existed but here the March Angling Association is shown in 1907 after they had won the March and Wisbech Inter-Club Shield for the third consecutive season. Back row: H. Smith, C. Fox, A. Reynolds, J. Cox (sen), A.C. Turner, G. Marshall. Front row: A. Fuller, F.W. Brundell, J. Tyler, C.S. Morris and S. Jackson.

Bowls has often been considered to be an 'old man's' game but in this team a number of younger players may be seen. The photograph, taken in the 1920s shows the team proudly displaying their recently acquired trophy. Back row, left to right: G. Inglett, H. R. Mallett, H.A. House, W. Wright, -?-, 'Kimbo' Smith. Front row: H. Baines, T. Cave, A. Broom, G.A. Turner, -?-, H.A. Cook.

The March Swimming Club men's Water Polo Team were successful in winning, for the second year, the Championship of the Isle of Ely and West Norfolk Water Polo League in 1934. The team consisted of, back row: Mr C. Hudson (referee), F.S. Edgar (goalkeeper), Geo Whittlesea (right back), G.W. Stevens (centre half), A.C. Bonnett (left back). Front row: H. Martin (right wing), P.A. Button (left wing) and N. Sproston (centre forward). On the end is R.H. Long who played, in place of Martin, against Kings Lynn.

The ladies of March Swimming club pose for their photograph in 1936. Back row, left to right: Mollie Woolhouse, Pat Reading, Gwenda Cheesewright, ? Cheesewright. Front row: ? Lockwood, Lucy Moss, Joan Collingwood and Madge Reading.

March Motorcycle Club about to leave on a day's outing in High Street at the junction with Burrowmoor Road. The bus in the background is patiently waiting for the photograph to be taken so it can then proceed to Chatteris.

March Wheelers Cycle Club pose for an official club photograph behind the George and Star in Broad Street, 1950. Up to forty members would cycle as far as Great Yarmouth or Melton Mowbray for a full day's ride or to Hunstanton for an afternoon or evening run. Following a day's outing, the club members would meet outside St Wendreda's church and cycle through town en masse. Back row: Dennis Searle, Tony Hill, Maurice Riches, Peter Hall, Donald Mennell, Maurice Larham, Henry Bond, Malcolm Davis and Norman Mansfield. Second row: Derek Watson, Fred Barker, David Pentney, Victor Stokes, Peggy Saywell, Joy Bell, Brian Fitt, Kath Dring, Kathy Curtis, Ray Bond, Brian Bent, John Cartwright, Sidney Butters and Mr Curry (Sen). Third row: Hugh Lemmon, Jeff Curry, Mr Cowlan (landlord of the George and Star), Mr Reginald Mallett (president), Len Bates, William Bates, ? Robinson and Colin Prince. Front row: Roland Westwood, Colin Bedford, Terry Westwood, John Mitcham, Paddy Overland, Brian Morton, Derek Wilson, Rodney Kilsby and Brian Gowler.

The ladies of the Evening Institute Keep Fit Group pose, for the photographer behind the Hereward School building in Robingoodfellows Lane, c. 1965. From the top of the steps are: Barbara Feary, Mavis Woolard, Freda Feary, Barbara White, Bridget Garwood, Sue Marriott, Enid Burbridge, Pat Ladds, -?- , Janet Gray, Carol Randall, Pat Bridgment, Joan Bull -?- , -?- .

Skating has always been a popular sport in the Fens and, while not a regular event due to the weather, every available opportunity is taken to practise. During the winter of 1963 freezing conditions prevailed for several months which led to some of the locals skating on the river through March.

Twelve
Bands and Groups

March Railway Prize Band photographed in front of the Band Room behind March Station in 1909. The conductor was Mr C. Steel, centre middle row, and the president of the band was Mr C. Crisp, centre in the front row.

March Imperial Band, later to become the March Town Silver Band, in 1925. The Imperial Band was easily identified by the piping on their uniform jackets.

The Salvation Army Band outside the Centenary Baptist chapel. The Salvation Army Band was formed in May 1908 under the direction of Mr Head. In the June of that year the Salvation Army, preceded by the band, marched to the market place for the first time.

March Town Band parading in the High Street in celebration of the Coronation of Queen Elizabeth II in 1953.

The Eastwood Avenue Jazz Band. Sixty performers gave a colourful and musical display at the celebrations for the Silver Jubilee of King George V in 1935. The band had been trained specially for the occasion by Messers S. Steward and L. Gotobed. Mrs Steward and Mrs Gotobed were responsible for most of the natty pierrot costumes.

Jock Dear's Band outside Harvey's fish shop, Dartford Road, in the 1950s. Jock Dear was a versatile local entertainer, much in demand.

Don Cowlan formed a small band before the Second World War supplemented by a few members of the Grammar School Orchestra. In Minden, Germany, during the war, he joined the Blue Anchors, a Navy band. When he left the forces, he formed a duo with his previous drummer and eventually could provide up to a twelve piece band for any dance or function. The band performed its final engagement at the GER Sports Club on New Year's Eve 1986. This 1941-42 band consisted of, from left to right, Doug Bristow (vocals), Cecil Bunting (sax), Bill Hammond (accordion), George Busk (trumpet), May Southon (accordion), Wally Mitchell (violin), Don Redhead (drums), Geo. Elgar (bass) and Don Cowlan (piano).

In October 1928 the March branch of the Isle of Ely Conservative Association organised a grand Empire Fair at the Palace Theatre. Members dressed to represent the different parts of the Empire and stalls selling Empire goods were designed to encourage people to support the Empire rather than 'foreign' goods. *The Cambridgeshire Times* stated that 'at night the various stalls were lit by electricity and the various shades enhanced the kaleidoscopic scene'.

St Peter's Church Literary Group performing *Little Mrs Cummin* in the Regent Theatre in 1933. On stage in a scene from the play are, from left to right: Mrs Forgan, Fred Ritchie, Mrs Stewart, Mr Hipwell, Mrs Peyton-Burbury, Mr Southerall and Ivy Morton. Also in the cast for this play, but off stage were John Burn, Nancy Whittome and Miss N. Upton.

March Choral Society singing in the Hippodrome in 1935. The Society flourished between the wars, giving two annual concerts, albeit with a rather limited repertoire. The guiding influence was Arnold Heathcote, Headmaster of the Grammar School.

A Liberal Party garden party in 1925. This was taking place at the home of Mr J. Bunkall, at Elwyn Orchard (behind the Griffin Hotel).

Miss Burrows and her Bible class. The grandfather of Miss Burrows, shown with glasses, donated part of his garden, at Hythe House (Audmoor House), High Street, to build a new Methodist chapel. The chapel has been refurbished and is now the Trinity church.

A celebration for the children of St Mary's Sunday school in the rectory garden in 1898. The rectory, in Westry, was burned down on Sunday 21 May 1978 when in private ownership.

A Methodist church outing in 1915. It was quite usual for industrial barges to be used for pleasure at the weekends and special occasions. Clean sacks were placed over the sides to keep the clothes of the passengers from getting soiled.

St Peter's church choir in 1950. In front of the Revd F.G. Breed, who came to St Peter's church before the Second World War, is the choirmaster Mr J.H. Burn.

Thirteen

Groups and Uniformed Organisations

March Auxiliary Fire Service with their two trailer pumps outside the Cock Inn, High Street, in early wartime. Ewart S. Pythian, landlord of the Cock, stands on the right.

The Fire Brigade outside the fire engine house on the Market Square in 1892. The fire engine, steam powered but still horse pulled, had a 40hp engine by Shand and Mason and carried half a mile of leather and canvas hose. This appliance was sold to Haddenham, Cambs, in November 1934 for £15, having served March for sixty-one years.

March Fire Brigade with a new motor driven fire engine probably in 1935. Back row, left to right: D. Gray, C. Goakes, G. Rowell, F. Steed, F. Doncaster, E. Turner, C. Goakes (sen.) and C. Washington. Front row: -?- , J. Collingwood, H. Bond, H. Bond (captain), F. Winterton, A. Emery and J. Hopper.

March Scout Group off to a County Rally at Cambridge in 1928.

March Scouts at a local Rally in Gaul Road recreation field in 1931. Mr H.R. Mallett, seen with his medals, was the Scout Master.

First March Brownies, c. 1931. Back row, left to right: Ellinton, -?- ,Mason and Youles. Middle row: Joan Tharby, Joan Utteridge, Freda Banham, Irene Watson and Joyce Emery. Front row: Hazel Bromley, Joyce Pratt, Gwen Nicholson and Pat Downes.

March Brownies and Guides on 'Thinking Day' in 1940.

The March GER St John Ambulance team. They were the winners of the Inter-Railway Shield in 1903 and 1904 and the GER Ambulance Cup in 1903, 1904 and 1906. Here, in 1907, they display both the shield and the cup which they have just won again. The team was, left to right: A.E. Mortlock, F.W. Brundell, W.L. Tabbitt, F. Watts and W. Goodley, Chief Officer. Back row, standing: J. Ablitt (Station Master), S.R. Beales, (Hon Sec.), C. Crisp, Loco Superintendent and Dr C.P. O'Connor, (Hon Surgeon).

March St John's Ambulance Ladies, with the Doctors Hislop, proudly display a newly acquired cup in 1938. From the back left: E. Heaton, E. Yardy, V. Caslake, ? Dunham, I. Bidwell and M. Russell; G. Ringham, E. Evans, -?-, -?-, ? English, E. Christmas, H. Green and E .Brewer; -?-, -?-, Dr Hislop, Mrs Shepperson, Dr M. Hislop, L.E. Lefevre and ? Dunham.

The 1947 St John Ambulance team continue the success of their 1907 predecessors and display, left to right, the East Anglian Cup, the Symons Eccles Cup and the GER Directors Cup. The team consists of D/O N. Sproston (Capt.), S. Jennings, A. Larham, T. Clingo (Instructor), F. Moore, F. Fairclough and S. Atkinson (Capt. Railway Team).

St John's Ambulance Nursing Cadet team, winners of the East Anglian Cadet Trophy held in Ely in 1945. The team was, from left to right: Barbara Hall, Margaret Bedford, Betty Watts, Dorothy Marie Smith and Eileen Lemon. Standing behind on the left are Mr S. Atkinson and Mr F. Fairclough.

The British Red Cross Society demonstrating their skills at a 'field hospital' in 1950.

Women's Co-operative Guild, adult class at the Co-op Hall in 1912. The Peterborough & District Co-operative shop and hall was demolished in the late 1980s to make way for Jim Hocking Court.

Staff of the Eastern Counties bus depot in Wisbech Road in the 1940s. This bus company, together with the Bluebell Bus Co., were the main means of road travel in the area.

The staff of Green's Nursery, situated in St Peter's Road, in 1906. The nursery was on the site of an old work house. Stan Green, seen on the extreme right, was famous for his magnificent carnations.

Fourteen
Agriculture

'Dockey Time'. A meal break taken in the fields either at 10.30 or 11 a.m., depending on which district you were working in. The word 'Dockey' referred to the fact that the farmer would reduce the wages (dock your money) for the time which was spent not working. Here the refreshment is being taken sitting beside a partially built corn stack in the 1930s.

Pea pickers at Peas Hill, March, in the mid-1930s. Pickers were paid by the number of bags they filled during the day. Nowadays peas are harvested mechanically with a viner or combined harvester. The photograph shows Mr and Mrs Longmire, Mrs Wooton and child and Mrs M. Sayer.

One of the first tractors used in area. C 1920s

A Titan tractor, first manufactured in 1918, is shown in the early 1920s, one of the first 'mechanical horses' to be used in the area. Note the steel wheels; tyres on tractors were not introduced until the late 1930s.

A Deering binder, used for cutting and tying corn. Three horses were needed to pull this machine round the field. Once the corn had been cut and tied into sheaves, farm labourers would stack them, eight or ten sheaves together in inverted Vs, locally called shocks, so the corn could dry before being transported to the large corn stacks. Binders were in regular use until the first combined harvesters were introduced in the early 1940s.

A Ford F tractor of 1918 vintage, has replaced the three horses on a Deering binder.

Betts threshing tackle in the mid-1930s. Mr Betts was a local contractor who travelled from farm to farm threshing corn, usually with the help of at least eleven farm hands. It was a very dusty and hard job. The Clayton & Shuttleworth threshing drum in the photograph is being driven by a belt attached to the steam engine.

Corn stacks at Morton's Farm, Hook near Wimblington. These are fine examples of the stacker's and thatcher's skills. Corn was stacked after harvest, usually near the farm yard, ready for threshing at a later date.